Jack Donaldson, later Lord Donald
these letters to his wife Frances (Fr:
War. They give a vivid picture of an
from Normandy to Egypt, then to]
into Europe for the final push of th

Rose Deakin, daughter of Frankie and Jack and aged 2-7 during the war, has edited these letters.

Jack Donaldson: A Soldier's Letters
On maintaining supply lines in the Second World War

Rose Deakin

Copyright © 2017 by **Rose Deakin**

All rights reserved. No part of this publication may be reproduced, distributed or transmitted in any form or by any means, without prior written permission.
Most of the photographs used are personal, from the family album. Every effort has been made to trace copyright or gain permission for use of the few that are not.

Rose Deakin
Published by: EVE – Eden Valley Editions
1 Fircroft Way
Edenbridge,
Kent TN8 6EL
Tel: +44 01732 863 939
www.eveeditions.com
Email: eve@topfoto.co.uk

Cover Design by Fred Deakin

Front cover photograph: Jack and Frankie Donaldson, by Denis Healey (with kind permission of the Healey family)

ISBN: 978-0-9929723-7-0

Website: womanswar.com

Email: rosedeakin@gmail.com

Contents

Foreword 1
1: In Normandy before Dunkirk 3
2: Egypt then Tobruk 16
3: Iraq 25
4: Persia, Tehran & the Russians 30
5: Cairo, planning for Italy 45
6: Italy and up through Europe 47
7: D Day and after 61

Foreword

Jack Donaldson was 31 when the Second World War broke out in September 1939. He had been married to Frankie for 4 years. They had 2 children: Thomas aged 3 and Rose aged 1 year and 10 months.

Educated at Eton and Cambridge, Jack had become a socialist in 1926, after what he observed during the General Strike. He came from a Conservative family, with a religious and public service background.

Jack joined the Royal Artillery (the Sappers) immediately war was declared and was abroad for most of its 6 years, working in logistics, supplies and troop movement. His most important war work was in Iran where he ran supplies for Russia. At that date Russia was under siege from Germany and, with no access through Europe, a supply line was set up in Iran, where Jack was posted. In 1943 he was summoned to Cairo to help with planning the invasion of Italy via Sicily.

After the war he returned to take up farming with Frankie (see **Frances Donaldson: A Woman's War**). *Always involved in politics, with a special interest in prison reform, he became a Labour peer in 1967 and was later Under-Secretary for Northern Ireland and then Minister for the Arts. He died in 1998.*

I edited Frankie's letters to him into 'A Woman's War'; a woman, on her own, battling to be a successful farmer in a man's world. However, while organising my mother's letters, and reading his, I began to realise that although his work was not in the front line actually killing the enemy or parachuting into Yugoslavia like my late father-in- law, his role was nonetheless both interesting and vital. I hope these letters help to give a picture of it.

His experience, very different from hers, reflected in his letters to her, tell a soldier's story; with striking immediacy. What was war really like for a mid-level officer on service in those years? One somewhat unexpected aspect of his war is that although it was both gruelling much of the time and sometimes dangerous, there was also plenty of time for social life. The officer class, especially in Cairo, had an extraordinary level of social interaction and nearly 'everyone' passed through at some point. Then in Iran it was the Russians, where part of his job was to get on with them and improve relations. The parties and meetings, even a Quartet Society which he set up in Italy after its invasion, contrast strongly with Frankie's loneliness in England.

Jack never talked about the war except when, 50 years after the end of the war, slightly deluded, in his last month or so of life, he suddenly asked me, "Who is my commanding officer?" When I looked blank he added, "Under whose instructions am I?" Clearly the war had had more impact on him than we had realised.

Although we all knew that he had a Russian medal, we never had the faintest idea of why or what his job had been. We weren't interested enough to inquire. His task was supply and logistics. When Evelyn Waugh, our country neighbour in the 50s, held a garden fete at his house, Colonel Donaldson was summoned to organise the car park because of his role in transport in the war!

Names are scattered around. I give surnames where I recognise them, but many of his war colleagues are not known to me. Jack and Frankie used a code when referring to Russia and politics as Jack was afraid of discrimination over his politics. Indeed, at one moment there was a suggestion that that might be taking place, but he emerged unscathed. The code for the Russians was "Bill's friends" and for the Americans "Johnnie's friends".

1: In Normandy before Dunkirk

War was declared on September 3rd, 1939. Jack left immediately. He went first to Yorkshire for training and then in November 1939 was sent to Normandy to organize movements at a local railway station (Abancourt). The Ribbentrop-Molotov Pact had been signed in August 1939 alongside a public non-aggression pact between Russia and Germany. This explains much of the distrust of Russia.

8/9/39 Weaver's Down.
Very busy dirty day, starting early to-morrow. We go for several days to a training camp and don't move up to our positions straight away. Apart from emotion, I'm in good form and really quite enjoying it all, and looking forward to the move and getting out of this blasted camp.

10/9/39
About to embark, sitting on the dock-side. Everyone in very good form, but all looking too ridiculous, with about 30lbs of equipment, haversack, tin hat, revolver, pack, rations etc., hanging all over us; and gas-masks and gas-capes to boot. We all look like travelling tinkers. It feels rather grand and heroic going "overseas", but for us of course it is a complete fraud, as I should think the port we're in now will be much more dangerous if the war perks up than anywhere we're likely to go.

11/9/39
I broke all rules by posting a letter to you last night, as the post-mark would give away where we are to a spy. Now, quite sensibly, I suppose, we are not allowed to post letters, and there is no postal service going, so I suppose it will be some days before you get this. We got in about 7 last night, and found ourselves very comfortable indeed, in a very decent 2nd class hotel, with an

immediate and wonderful hot bath, good simple French food, a room to myself and a change of clothes. Our men are very comfortably billeted in a school, and we now settle down, I expect, to a week of drill and things like that. My section-commander is on a trip, which leaves me in command of one of the 2 sections, which will mean a little to do. This hotel is full of officers, and, what was rather sweet, there was an air-raid warning last night through which every single one slept soundly. As soon as we get settled anywhere, I shall ask you to send me Hogben's Mathematics for the Million, and the Left Book Club National Capitalism. If only we weren't separated it would be a very nice war so far.

12/9/39
Still nothing has been done about post, but I'll keep up with what news there is and post them altogether. We were the first troops to march through this town which is rather sweet, as they are the most unwarlike group of clerks and railway porters you could imagine, but they did it very well. The whole thing becomes increasingly comic opera.

16/9/39
I've just heard the best news I've heard since I got out here, that I can at last write to you, so long as I give no information whatever. I've already written 3 letters which I am now sending. Last night and the night before I dined with Ralph *(Jarvis, a school friend)* and Bobby Mackenzie, and to-night with Ralph and Bob Laycock *(a commando general)*, so from the social point of view it is all rather fun. I should be quite happy if you were here. I long to hear from you. I expect letters will begin to get through soon.

Will you send me the New Statesman?

18/9/39
The more I think about things, the more I think, if we ever get back again and settled down, we'd better seriously try to take up

farming. I know that I don't really want anything from life but to be with you and the children and work together at home, and I can't see what else we can work at.

Think about it seriously. We would presumably sell the house and go further out somewhere, putting say half our money in land and fittings and saving the other half to live on meanwhile, if any is left after the war, that is to say. When we get together again, I don't want to spend ten hours a day away from home if I can help it. Life is too short and our union too close for that to make sense.

It will be lovely to hear from you again. It leaves me completely half-dead not to. However, the half which is left continues to function quite efficiently and even gaily, so I suppose we mustn't grumble.

By the way, I gather that we get £2.2/- a week marriage allowance, and my pay is about £6 a week, of which I oughtn't to spend more than £2, so we shall not starve on that account.

My deep-rooted fear seems to be for the world more than for you and me and the children, and tho' the world may perish, which would be a pity and which we must try to stop, yet I don't think <u>we</u> shall, in our present circumstances.

1/10/39
Well, the first two trains went off alright last night in lovely moonlight (at 8 p.m. and 1 p.m.); and the third last night at also in lovely moonlight. We got through them very well and I left at 7, getting up at 6 this morning, very well pleased to find the job was easy and I could do it. I drank hot red wine with the stationmaster and shunters last night before going to bed, and altogether had a lovely time, and of course loved all the station staff.

7/10/39
I wish you could get a job ... you'd be much better ... but don't think I mind getting gloomy letters. I want to hear from you as

you are and not as you think I'd like you to be. It is far harder for you living the same life almost than for me who am meeting quite new problems all the time. You speak in your last letter of a "farm scheme". I imagine all this links up with your and my scheme of putting our capital into land and house, which I still agree with. In a week or two we shall be properly in cross-correspondence and can discuss details. What you do will be right for me my darling whatever it is. I'd much rather you chose without me than I without you for our future's sake, as I back your judgment much more than mine.

The great thing is to be busy, so I'm frightfully keen on your farm scheme, whatever it is (that letter is missing), for that reason as much as any.

10/10/39
This is what is called a regulating station, and every train which goes forward is labelled to here in code. We have to check the wagons, relabel in clear to the correct destination, and group the wagons so as to avoid shunting further up the line. For the first few days the muddle was unbelievable. We were bunged down here at lunchtime and started work at 6, with no clear idea of what was likely to happen, no office and no experience. Trains arrived at all hours, without any warning whatever, wrongly labelled and stuffed like packs of cards. We had to sort out the whole thing, taking sometimes as much as 3 hours to shunt a train which was supposed to leave in 8 minutes, with the French tearing their hair because they wanted the line cleared.

Now it is all going quite well. We're getting proper advice of trains so that we know what is coming and can tell the station-master what to be ready for, and the trains are reaching us better marshalled. The first struggle was really great fun, as it was a real fight against difficulties, mostly in pitch darkness in a large railway yard with men so inexperienced they copied wagon numbers down wrong. However, we did jolly well and didn't make a single bloomer. I got 3 hours sleep the first night, 6 the second and about 3 the third. I took it as rather a compliment to be sent in charge here and am very pleased that we've so far made a good job of it.

14/10/39
We're trying to commandeer the local chateau, a brand new building with a bath and 2 lavatories and central heating, which ahs never been lived in and only built 3 years. I went up and interviewed the owner who, with his wife and son, was quite pleasan. The next morning at 8 o'clock he turned up to say it was not "commode" after all for us to have it. So I brought him in to see the French captain who deals with these things, whom he rubbed up the wrong way thoroughly. The Capitaine, after he'd gone, said "I'm going to have that off him even if you don't want it." Which is of course the right spirit. It turned out afterwards that he is ill and a little mad, and his wife was charming and delighted for us to have it, only hoping he won't make a scene and get arrested.

...Later: As I told you this morning, I've been busy trying to snaffle the local chateau, and I think we're going to get away with it. It would be wonderful to have a clean lavatory again, and a bath. I got a bath this morning, the first for 8 days, in the place reserved for the "mechaniciens", engine-drivers etc. It was piping hot and quite clean and I feel a new man.

Work continues to go well. So far we haven't made a bloomer. Everything that goes forward goes through us, and we turned over 800 wagons in the first week. It is really just like playing trains.

11/11/39
As to the house *(they had commissioned Walter Gropius to build their family house in 1935 when they married)*, I'm not a bit interested what other people think. Gropius has more genuine feeling in his little finger than Serge in his whole body, and the house , as a modest

bourgeois house built with some regard to income, is a much better whole than anything Serge (Chermayeff) would ever do, even though I'm very fond of Serge's house. Don't worry. I'm quite confident it would let, even if it took a long time and got a bad rent. But the whole 'folly' idea is nonsense. It is certainly one of the best things we have done, and I'm very proud of it and f--- them all.

Many of Jack's friends hated the Gropius house that he and Frankie had built, and called it 'the chicken shed'.

27/11/39

I'm busy today because we have a party of 13 officers and 21 NCOs from Base Area M.C. Groups coming to see our Regulating Station. I want to make the work here look as complex as possible. Luckily we've got a fairly full yard, and a train of 64 wagons to go out to-night, made up from different in-coming trains, so it will look quite good. Buchanan, who's going to lecture them for half an hour on the functions of Regn. Stn., is coming down any minute to be told what they are.

1/12/39

I had an absurd but very pleasant evening with Ralph *(Jarvis)* last night. He's in very jovial form, and on Christian names with all the best people, all very public school and mostly last generation, who seem to man the intelligence. He turned up with tickets for a show given by Leslie Henson, Binnie Barnes and Violet Lorraine, which was really quite enjoyable. I found V.L. singing "If you were the only girl;" rather moving. I sat 2 away from Gerry Wellesley, who, having never seen a uniform before, has turned up as a major in the Guards in Ralph's sort of work.

The O.E *(Old Etonian)* party was the most embarrassing thing I've ever been to. There were 8 officers, all from the same section of work (Ralph's) all over 40 bar Anthony Eden's brother and one contemporary of ours called Barnett, and all knowing each other extremely well. Eddie Grant was there, but no-one else I knew. Ralph, who knew them all a bit was somewhat embarrassed, and I was acutely uncomfortable, being unknown and unwanted. However it all warmed up with a few bottles of champagne, and we ended by singing the Boating Song over and over again very loud indeed with a drunken captain conducting and refusing to let us stop.

I felt rather glad to be isolated in this job and not to be Ralph. I don't quite know why, but I find highly cultured and educated and upper-class companions rather a bore, and he has nothing else.

6/12/39

The party at the sergeants' mess was much like other parties of that sort, but not bad. We all got a bit tight and I woke up with something of a head. Things were busy when I got here and I had no time to relax before we all went to lunch with the station master at 1.30. This was a true epic. There were the two French officers and Greenhill and me and one of the station employees and his wife, and M. & Mme Racine.

We started with 2 glasses of byrrh as aperitif, (a deux jambes!) and some pleasant hors-d'oeuvres. Then Coquille St.Jacques, which is a sort of scallop and very good. With this a very dray white Burgundy. Then the most delicious pigeon, roast with butter and a little brandy, one of the finest flavours I've tasted, and with it some excellent red Chateau neuf du Pape 1934. Then an old Norman custom i.e. a glass of Calvados all round "pour faire couler" so that you can start the next course without feeling jaded. then roast chicken and the most beautiful stuffing, and a separate course of roast tiny potatoes. With this, some lovely red Moulin a Vent Burgundy 1933, then cheese and more Chateauneuf, then an exquisite apple tart, with a sweet Grave, then coffee and Cognac and more Calvados.

We got up weakly about 4 after one of the best meals I've ever eaten, only to hear Mme Racine insisting that we all come back to supper at 7! Which we did, and staggered home at 10.30 physically exhausted.

They are quite charming people and all very nice indeed. the employee's wife obviously acted as a maid and help to Mme but sat down with us after waiting on us, and it was all very good in that way, yet they are probably violently anti-socialist.

7/12/39

I'm afraid I can no longer defend Russia. I think they've done themselves a bit of harm, however, by really shocking everyone, and, after all, the loss of support of millions of people who thought as I did even must amount to something. It's the biggest let-down in history, and one finds the French workers one talks to very bitter about it. It seems to me to have completely put out of court any <u>communist</u> revolution in any country where the papers are reasonably uncontrolled. One must be careful not to let hate of existing institutions drive one anywhere at the present time, as it does really seem as if we maligned the government over the Anglo-Soviet negotiations.

You must watch this white feather business. One really ought to be grateful to people like Walter for restoring one's amour-propre. John L is a much more interesting case. He's a very tough chap and certainly no coward. I suppose he just thinks the whole thing a bore and is buggered if he's going to get mixed up with it before he has to. Which I respect, but he ought to say so.

Jack was very pro-Russian, as were some other idealistic young Englishmen of the 30's, reacting against the poverty and almost feudalistic society of England at that time. Hunger marches and so on. (See also 'Radiant Illusion?', a book of essays on this topic edited by Nicholas Deakin)

However, he was shattered when Russia invaded Finland. He wrote this letter to the New Statesman but it was not sent – possibly Frankie's decision.

10/12/39   Letter to the New Statesman

Sir,

Recantations of the least significant people may be worth publishing. I wish to state publicly that my past admiration for the achievements of Russia, and consequent sympathy with her friends in England, is turned to disgust. Almost every argument used against the fascists in Spain applies against the Russians in Finland. The arguments were true then and they are true now.

We shall miss the Communists, when the Nazi menace has been dealt with and we can turn to the attempt to do something better.

We shall miss their courage and energy, and for the people of Britain it is galling to lose good allies to anything as squalid as Stalin's new imperialism.

But it won't do. Judgment cannot be sound in people who can swallow the liquidation of the Kulaks, the shooting of the generals, the trials of the old Bolsheviks and now (for me the final emetic) the attack on Finland, and continue to believe the author of all these slaughters is the champion of the common man throughout the world. Perhaps such obstinate blindness counterbalances the courage and energy and perhaps we are better without them.

Labour leaders have thought so for years. I have not. Now I recant, and I say let us judge the sincerity of our friends' allegiance to working-class ideals by the speed with which they dissociate themselves from Stalin and his adherents over here.

I am, sir etc.

Everything seemed quiet and humdrum for a month or two. Then in April 1940 Nazis invade Denmark and Norway.

9/4/40

Well, bang goes Denmark and most of Norway. The 6 o'clock news says a naval battle is in progress. I hope to God we swipe the buggers. When he moves, one has to admit that he moves bloody quick --- a marvellous show. I hope we succeed in doing something effective to help the wretched Norwegians. Otherwise I suppose our own food situation may become serious. I wonder if it will stop leave. Let's hope anyway, and I don't suppose it would be for very long. I can't help feeling rather pleased that things are moving. It must bring it nearer to an end and will infuriate Americans and all neutrals.

14/4/40

A letter to-day, finally clinching the farm. You've been terrific in snap and decision. It's always right to go against the strong opinion of an expert.

25/5/40

Well and fit and really rather enjoying a slightly more active war. You'll have gathered that the Bosch occupation of Amiens made our position untenable. So we evacuated in an orderly and decent way, and are now a sort of self-contained mobile unit of which I'm the boss. It's all rather fun, a change and rather more adventurous, tho' scarcely more dangerous. The morale, particularly among civilian French, having been extremely low and quite difficult to cope with, is now very much better and everybody's feeling fierce and damned if the bugger shall get away with it. I'm more confident of winning than I've been for years, tho' I think it may take a long time.

May 26, Evacuation of Allied troops from Dunkirk begins. This marks the end of the Phoney War. There was a serious threat of invasion and Jack wrote discussing what Frankie should do if it happened.

29/5/40

I'm afraid they're certain to try to invade England. If they do, you've just got to stay put. Should just stay on the farm, either Mary's or ours, and look as natural to the neighbourhood as possible. It sounds absurd to think they'd ever get anywhere near you, but everybody felt perfectly safe in Amiens and they were wrong.

The first thing is not to be on the roads, and the second is to have food. In the event of complete chaos and our getting separated and unable to meet, I'd go to Lloyds Bank, St James's St. to get your address. Failing that I'd try all friends. Failing that I would go to the entrance of Gypsy Hall on the first of every month, from 12 till 2pm. Failing that to the pub at Shipbourne on the 10th of every month, same hours. Failing that, St Martin's in the Fields, steps Trafalgar Square 6-7am, 12-1pm and 9-10pm. If Norfolk were a clear area, I'd go to Runton *(their holiday house)...* If only the north were clear, I'd aim for Witherslack *(home of Maureen and Oliver Stanley)...* I hope all this is the most idiotic fantasy but intellectually I think it is a very real possibility. Remember that death will re-unite us.

2/6/40

We're obviously taking incredible punishment, but it doesn't seem to have affected our will to win. I'm still busy on a night-loading job. I'm well and happy and rather enjoy the more active war conditions.

3/6/40

The very fine show put up by the BEF in their evacuation has gone a long way to restore prestige. The wireless says 4/5ths are already in England. We had rather an exciting time evacuating the old place. I'll tell you all about it when we meet --- it's probably meat for the censor if I write it here. You needn't worry at all about railway bombing. Unless one falls actually on you, it is quite harmless and unfrightening. I've been near it only once and found it quite stimulating. Bombing is only frightening and dangerous in a town or where there are masses of troops. It is completely wasted on isolated railheads. We've already learnt enough not to be optimistic, and I have fairly faced the worst as I'm sure you have. So almost any change will be for the better.

10/6/40

We've had a fairly exciting and slightly harassing time for the last few weeks, as you can imagine. I'm sitting in a lovely orchard in lovely weather and the most lovely thing has happened. A sergeant who used to be with me has just turned up from a neighbouring post and brought with him a letter from you. It says you've got my letters after the Amiens show, which I knew would be your worst period.

Now darling I want you to think this over very carefully. I want to try to get transferred out of this to the artillery. My reasons are as follows: a) I've twice been within 15 miles of the Bosch and each time had to skip in a rather undignified manner, being absolutely without any means of defence. I <u>must</u> get into something where I can anyway feel I am hitting back. b) This is the great crisis. I want to take an active share in it.

I've very nearly done it on my own bat, but I thought it would not be fair so I'm going to wait for your OK. Be honest --- if you really feel it would be too much hell, you and the family come first, and I'll do what you want. But it would be nice to be able to hit back a bit and feel one was doing the maximum, instead of flapping around, which is all we seem to do in a crisis.

I am so radiantly pleased to have heard from and above all to know that my cosy feeling about you and the farm and the children is not shattered by a lot of bone-headed solicitors and bank managers and stockbrokers.

16/10/40 (Back in England after Dunkirk)

A teleprint came in this morning saying "Major Donaldson selected as DADTN No 8 Group". I shall have a week's embarkation leave, probably next week. Now, sweetie, this is pretty bad for both of us. I know how you feel and you know how I feel. But it's better than last time.

I have not been able to find out what DADTN stands for. Possibly Deputy Assistant Director Transport. But N?

To begin with, the war is nearer the end. Secondly it's a lovely job for me, really. And thirdly, you've got the farm to lose yourself in. It will be Egypt, almost certainly. Anyway, there's a war on, and this is what one enlisted for. I hope you'll help me by being very tough over it. You know how I get, and I need all your help.

2: Egypt then Tobruk

16/10/40
We've got to face at the worst 6 weeks, at the best a month without communication. We must sleep and work thro' it and then that one will be over and we can try and find something else to work thro' to.

Movement Control GHQ Middle East   3/1/41
Well, my love, here I am in the second best hotel permanently attached to MC GHQ and likely to stay here for the rest of the war. I'm very disappointed, in a way, because I had really hoped to go to the Western Desert and see a bit of fun, but of course there are compensations. Beginning again is always pretty frightful and I had hoped to be sent somewhere with a little more scope for initiative. This is very much a country not at war. It's all quite interesting. I'm going to try to learn some Arabic and meet some Egyptians.

4/1/41
I've done a day's work at GHQ. Not unlike Darlington with knobs on. I saw Robert Adeane for a second. Oddly enough, I'm going to work in the same room as Eric Sandars who was at school and played the drums in the Cambridge band. We work odd hours, 8.15 - 1.30 and 5.30 - 7.30 (usually later). So there's fair time for tennis, which I shall try to do regularly, and also take Arabic lessons. I'm somewhat depressed, which I always am starting anything. I hope you get a cable soon. I shall post about twice a week.

6/1/41
At the moment I'm lonely and bored. I dined with Robert *(?ADeane)* last night. He's got a very exotic flat and an excellent

black servant. That is the way to live, and for two is cheaper. I shall join the Gezira sporting club for tennis and bathing, but it costs £2 for three months and I shall have to buy white shorts etc. I'm afraid I'm inevitably going to spend a bit settling in, but I'll be as careful as I can and I assure you I get no fun out of anything.

I wired you again giving correct address, so perhaps soon I may hear a word from you. Poor old wops, they <u>have</u> taken a pasting --- 35,000 prisoners more. It poses quite a Movement control problem.

Canal Base Area Middle East   15/1/41

I spent the last 2 1/2 days driving round and looking at this area. I'm sent down here as DADTN Canal Area (for a month) and it presents some quite amusing railway problems, and quite difficult ones too. *(Humphrey)* Lomer and Shillaker and Hoffman *(army colleagues)* are each in charge of sub-areas covered by this area. So I have to co-ordinate and regulate their various requirements.

This is the sort of thing I at any rate think I can do, and as it needs doing very badly it ought to be fun. I live in a very nice house; there is a Lt. Colonel in charge, called Thicknesse, who is very charming and probably brilliant, but never stops talking rather like Cecil Beaton. Then there are two captains, Brown, very nice, scholar of Balliol, and Wilson, who is rather silly (all girls together) but harmless and pleasant, and a very handsome young lieutenant called Harris. A friendly but rather gushing mess. I'm very happy to have got away from GHQ and to have a real job of work to do.

21/1/41

Life is very hectic. It's hard to get a move on but I think things are moving a little bit. The mess is rather good. There's a very good black servant called Mahomet, who has never gone below a brigadier before, a good black cook, and two other helps. There's a Buick with Abdul to drive, whisky and gin bought wholesale, each having our own bottle on the sideboard. The poor Egyptians, tho' completely down-trodden, are very strong physically, and have got good physical endurance. In every group of 100 you'll find one who works hard and is clever. It's a lower proportion than with us, but I shouldn't think it's lower than it was among the "villeins and serfs" in feudal times. Yet those were the stock which has produced the British working man.

It is clear that as long as this sort of people is run by the British, they will never learn to run themselves, so the sooner we get out the better. We've got out of here, and things are already beginning to go not so well as when we were here. But I don't think the average wog cares the least. Islam at its present stage is a very reactionary religion. I wish I had time to go on with my Arabic. Anyway, I feel certain Egypt would have been a better place if we had never come here. --- not a more civilized place, but a place with a more unified civilization. There would only have been their own feudal oriental exploitation, instead of the commercialism which they do so well and so ruthlessly once they have learnt the rules. It will be harder to upset than their own natural development, and therefore progress will be more difficult.

26/1/41
The Egyptians are quite extraordinary. They always give you the answer you want, whether true or not. I spent all yesterday tracing a train of empty wagons from one place to another, and got reports of it passing here at such and such a time, and having engine trouble there etc. In the end it turned out that it had never started, the wagons having been sent in the opposite direction.

The Egyptians are simply wonderful. They bow and smile and say yes to every suggestion. If you look really determined, they say they can't do this because .....etc. If you say alright, you'll remove that obstacle, they find another, and you have to remove that. Then you see a gleam of desperation in their eyes and finally if you pin them down and have removed every objection they will do it. But if they find a single difficulty they won't tell you. They'll say yes and not do it. When you ask them why, they'll give the obstacle as the reason. They are the result of ingrained centuries of despotism and bullying, where whatever you did got the bastinado, so it was probably better to do nothing you didn't absolutely have to. Trying to get things done in this way is a real art of which I'm not yet master, but getting better. How long it seems without a letter. I do wonder if you're getting mine yet.

24/2/41

A nice visit to Shepheard's, which is a very good. Coming out, who should I meet but Peter Fleming *(a commando, brother of Ian)* --- a major, without any unit, obviously going to do something frightfully hush-hush, probably in the Far East, I thought. Things seem to be blowing up towards a Balkan war alright.

27/3/41

The Commandant arrived yesterday, Brigadier Dorman-Smith, brother of the late Minister of Agriculture, but much more intelligent. Reputed to be brilliant. He spent four hours to-day lecturing us on the Western Desert campaign and explaining how it was governed all along by the question of supply.

1/4/41

I had rather an interesting evening on Sunday. I sat next to the Brigadier at supper, and we started talking about books, and then he started talking about my generation, and wondered whether it didn't lack something, so then we were well away and he asked me along to his room to go on talking. He then turned out to be a most intelligent and independent thinker. He's 45 and this is his second war. He's a soldier and has worked on salary all his life, so he knows the one about "no incentive without profit" is balls. He says there are a good many pretty good men like him, angry men, who feel this is the most blatantly unnecessary war that has ever been fought, that even microscopic integrity and intelligence in leadership could have avoided it; who are now adamant to see it through to the bitter end, but who are not prepared to have the whole thing wrecked again by selfishness, dishonesty, cowardice and the rest. They will stand by as long as the government, whatever it may be, seems progressive and just and sensible, but it if starts real nonsense they'll be perfectly prepared to get their guns, which they know how to use.

21/9/41
The only news is still the book.

Frankie had written a book about her farming experiences, and called it Approach to Farming.

The English and the style are both very good, and not noticeable, which is the great test, of course, like the gentlemen's clothes. I'm longing to know what Leonora *(Cazalet)* thinks.

I wonder if we're giving the Russians enough help? I feel Winston and the heads are probably doing all they can for them, but I should think there's a very thick lair of confirmed anti-Bolsheviks thro' which any action has to filter and where it can be very successfully delayed. What do people think?

21/12/41
I went to Cairo with the Colonel two days ago. At lunch at Shepheard's I told him of the letter I'd written to you about a possible move to the Welsh Guards. I said I was 100% certain you would veto it, but would rather like a change all the same. He said "They'd fight hard at HQ to stop you going". I said "I dare say. I know my value and you know yours. But it's absurd to say you couldn't find someone to do my job adequately in no time". He said "I can't think of a major or a Lt. Col. In the Middle East who would run the railway side at Suez as well as you have". Which I thought almost too flattering. It is embarrassing to pass on things like this but you asked for it.

25/12/41

I'm rather tight. A lot of things have happened since I wrote to you this morning. Halifax and Spilsbury are in hospital and organised a good party up there. We sent back to the mess for a bottle of gin to make our contribution. We had a drink or two, when the Colonel came in, saying he was the harbinger of bad news. a) Poor old Shillaker had been out on the jag for three days, and had finally been placed under close arrest. b) I am to be moved immediately to Tobruk. a) is a bad business, and is the end, I should think, of his army career. He's a really good chap, immensely able and full of guts, but when every so often he goes on a jag he's nobody's business. b) is of course very exciting and rather flattering for me.

They told the Colonel they must have a strong hand up there and couldn't think of anyone else. The interesting thing is that I'm supposed to be a railway specialist and there isn't a railway in miles. So I really do take it as a compliment. Tommy *(colleague)* was so distressed that he and I got pretty drunk before lunch. He said "I knew it was too good to last". I shall be very sorry to leave Tommy and the Colonel, to both of whom I am devoted. But I love change.

28/12/41

I've already told you I'm going to Tobruk. The position is that, when it was besieged, it just kept going under incredibly difficult conditions, with continual dive-bombing from Boche aerodromes only a few miles away, and the Movements job was done with unbelievable gallantry by an ex-regular sergeant-major, now a major, who was a by-word for coolness and courage and carrying on under great difficulties. But neither he nor the chaps with him, after a year's frightful strain, are necessarily the right people to develop the place now that the strain is over.

The anti-climax, after so long a strain and the relief, would not be the right background for steady development of the most important forward base in the western campaign. So they wanted someone good enough and stout enough to follow him, and at the same time with enough technical knowledge and drive to expand and improve the job. And that's me. All of which I take as a compliment. As far as I can see there's nothing frightfully difficult about it but shall be responsible for the whole place, from a movements points of view, under the Army HQ up there.

I complained to Randolph *(Churchill)* that his father only gave 20 seconds to Russia in a 35 minute speech. His reply was that they're all rather sick with Russia for not coming in against Japan

Russia was by now an ally having entered the war as our ally in June 1941.

Jack never managed to take up the job in Tobruk as he developed jaundice (hepatitis) and was in hospital for a long time. As a result he was posted to Iraq to work on that front and later to Iran to be in close contact with the Russians getting supplies round through the East to the beleaguered Leningrad and large parts of Russia.

6/1/42

The Tobruk hospital was incredible. I'm sure they find it very difficult to get supplies and everything is sunk and all that, but nothing but deliberate sadism could excuse its squalor. It's in an old but not badly bombed Italian hospital, with all doors and windows blown in. This has completely beaten them. They got as far as nailing a blanket over a door, but to nail two and put weights on their bottom was too much for them.

The day I arrived I was put into ward 9, a long room with about four doors and windows on each side, and everywhere blankets blowing horizontally into the room, and gaunt cowering figures trying to bore thro' their pillowless beds to escape the pitiless draught. The medical inspection was pretty funny. Two doors were in a straight line either side of the room, (horizontal blankets of course). You wouldn't credit it, but they placed the examination bed between the two and on it sat waiting patients. The food was minimal, not that I minded, the rain poured on to the bed next to mine, and it took actual physical threats to produce a cup of hot water to shave in. All thro' sheer hopeless incompetence, --- no ill will at all. In fairness, their job is not to treat, but to diagnose and evacuate. But all the same it was a bit over the odds.

Evacuation was held up by an air-raid, and it wasn't till 10 pm that we finally dressed and went down in an open ambulance to the docks. Here it was pouring with rain and blowing hard, and we had to get into open boats and be towed out to the hospital ship. By this time I was past caring, but when we finally got aboard we were treated to everything in the world.

The ship was a real paradise, exquisitely run with charming people running her. Now I have a comfortable room to myself and am quite content to be apathetic and get well in my own time. I don't feel well but not ill either. Anyway, now I'm here and eating the proper food it's no great hardship. My baggage was last heard of on the way to Torbruk by truck, and as it contains vols 2 and 3 of War and Peace, (and I'm getting towards the end of vol 1,) plus Hogben and my Arabic book, it's all rather a pity.

As to the job, I was upset at first, but since have been too ill to care. It may well be vacant still when I come out. I simply don't know.

30/1/42

I was chosen to go to Tobruk because it needed putting right, not because I'm an expert at dock-working. On the other hand, they will need chaps for the two places I told you Reggie Fellowes *(Jack's commanding officer for the Middle East period of his war)* is going to, ending in N & Q, (IraN and IraQ)and some of these would be railways jobs, so Thicknesse thinks I might go to one of them.

Leave is working out well. I'm going with Andrew Early and Peter Chance to Luxor on 2nd February, probably for a week. Than I shall probably spend two or three days in Cairo before going wherever I am going. I'm delighted not to know.

Winter Palace Hotel, Luxor 2/2/41

We had a good journey up last night. We went off in style, having the Assistant Traffic Manager (my old friend Abdul Rahim) and the Cairo Station superintendent (who used to be at Ismailia) to see us off, having reserved us a first-class carriage and put sheets and blankets and pillows in for us, thereby saving us 25/- each for a sleeper.

About 10 minutes before we left, who should turn up but Andrew Early (who I told you couldn't come at the last minute) and Reggie Fellowes, very smart as a full colonel. I was rather flattered, as he only arrived that day, and came along to ask if I would go along with him to the place ending in Q if he could fix it. I said I would love to, tho' I would still more like it to end in N. I would love to work with Reggie again. From your point of view I don't see that Q is much worse than Egypt and not so bad as Syria. *(IraN and IraQ)*

Bob Laycock, by the way, was missing for 40 days, but got back and is now in England, about to become a brigadier.

3: Iraq

Jack's Identity card for Egypt and the Middle East

15/2/42

Well, I have at last got my marching orders. I go to join Reggie and the shades of Haroun al Raschid at 6.30 am to-morrow by plane. *(Baghdad)*

19/2/42

We got here by air quite comfortably on the 16th. I've been pretty busy looking round ever since. The city of Haroun al Raschid is not too bad at first sight, and the work will be interesting, very like the beginning in Egypt.

My particular problem is introducing a proper system into the stores' traffic from here up to the various northern frontiers which is my area.

27/2/42

If you meet Stafford Cripps, tell him that the gossip (not first-hand) out here is that the diplomatic and consular people particularly mishandle the Russians, and the military are so gauche and awkward as to be positively rude. The Russian Military Mission was dumped in a 2nd class hotel in Baghdad, and no-one called on them after hours, while they had hoped for vodka and women and an English guide. Only gossip, but what a mess when one thinks that, but for them, we should be running like hares from all this part of the world. Admittedly the R.s are very difficult, grasping and incompetent in many ways, frightened of acting on their own without reference to the Kremlin, and altogether touchy and impossible, tho' friendly enough individually. But that's what diplomats are for, to deal with tricky situations. English people are so crass where their pride is concerned, and aren't nearly grateful enough for having their lives saved.

1/3/42

A very pleasant day yesterday. I drove over to Tripoli with Cliff Wood, a lovely drive. To-day, with a professional interest in railways, we decided to do the return journey from Beirut to Damascus by train. By car it takes 2 ½ hours, by train 11, but it was worth it. You wind up a rock-railway for 5 hours, 7 till 12, without ever losing sight of Beirut or the sea; then, having reached the top of the pass, the train descends gently to the plain, goes to Rayak, on quite a bit, makes into the foothills of the anti-Lebanon, turns a complete semi-circle and comes down the most heavenly gorge I've ever been in, for about 2 solid hours, into Damascus.

The apricot, peach and almond blossom was newly out: there was a rushing torrent at the bottom of the gorge, then 1/4 to ½ a mile cultivated with fruit trees in blossom, and a lot of trees looking like young ash, then sheer rock one side, desert hills the other, and the snow streaked anti-Lebanon as background. The peasants looked happy and charming, ruddy faced, gaily dressed but dirty, and delightful children. If you looked up the rock-face on the other side you saw an occasional flock of goats, black and hanging on by their eyebrows. Eleven hours well wasted. I thought it would be more fun to spend another night at Damascus rather than at Beirut.

2/3/42

I'm about to set off on a tour of Damascus. All I know of it is that it is the Palm Sunday town, and said to be the oldest inhabited city in the world. It has a lovely setting, hills close on one side and desert on the other, and the approach by train never seems to get out of an endless and exquisite orchard in full blossom. It seems the most sympathetic town, from the hotel window, that I've been to yet. One sees more people out of the Bible and other pasts here than in most places. Chaps with brown night-gowns and white turbans round their tarbush and a close shaved black beard. Trams and donkeys, lounge suits, Turkish trousers and nightgowns, all quite fun to look at.

I travelled through Syria in 1992 and looked for the valleys of peach and almond blossom but sadly they were all filled with concrete blocks and skyscrapers. Now they are almost certainly filled with rubble and dust.

22/3/42

The more I have to do with Iraqis and Indians the more I feel we should leave them alone as soon as we can after the war. We've ruled them and as such we are not the right people to hand over independence to them gradually. They irritate us and make us feel superior. We make them aggressive and difficult just because we have ruled them and are now relaxing the rule. And they can't manage our capitalism at all and make even more hash of it than we do.

The Anglo-Soviet invasion of Iran took place in August- September 1941. Paiforce (Persia and Iraq force) was made up of the 8th and 10th Indian Infantry divisions, some British forces and the 21st Indian Infantry Brigade.

17/4/42

I don't seem to have written to you for ages. I'm in a vile temper to-day. I hate the Indian Army and everything to do with it. It's the most dreadful buck-passing organization you can imagine, with almost two inefficient servants to every officer and damn nearly one to every sergeant. Really horrifying. I've had two very long letters complete mainly about your plans. I'm sure you'll be alright in whatever you do (except in the only once suggested idea of sending the children away, which you know I would never support or indeed allow). Anything, bar separation from the children, is justified to deal with the loneliness situation.

1/5/42

There's just an off-chance, I think, that Reggie might send me East on the aid to Uncle Joe racket. I've always meant to get there, and I've done about all I can here, and things are a little better.

19/5/42

The trouble with Movements is that, at my level, there's a job to do wherever you go getting the thing running properly, which one succeeds in to a limited extent (very limited here) within about two months. Then the work degenerates into a clerk's job. I'd really like to use my mind for a bit. One's contribution to the war effort is and has been very undistinguished. So far our army has lost four major campaigns, in Norway, Greece, France and Singapore. I've contributed to France and Greece, but have never had the satisfaction of being under fire even. I feel I might have been more use as a civilian, where one's abilities might have been more extended. Having done easy jobs well and given satisfaction to my superiors has blinded me to how undistinguished a role I have in fact played.

26/5/42

Reggie *(Fellowes)* is definitely putting me forward as AQMG Persia, which would be just what of all things I should have chosen. It will be exciting to live in Tehran and meet Russians and feel one is mixed up in that part of the job.

May 27, 1942 – SS Leader Heydrich attacked in Prague. Known as "the Hangman", he stood out as one of the most brutal mass murderers in Nazi Germany. He was attacked and died a few days later of his wounds.

8/6/42

We had a party for the death of Heydrich and I stood drinks all round.

Jack was now sent to Tehran to work directly with the Russians. As well as a wild social life (part of the job) there was very hard work. Jack was both clever and able and knew it. He was confident in himself and yet always felt he had not done enough. The parties all took place, yes, but in between the work was difficult, arduous and vitally important. Here he was trying to help break the Nazi domination of Europe and Russia. Later, when helping to plan and then supply the Italian invasion and move the army up through Europe, the pressure was even greater and he was often depressed, again always feeling that he had not done enough.

4: Persia, Tehran & the Russians

Movements c/o Transportation, Tehran   15/6/42
Here I am, where I always wanted to be. I suspected it would be a sticky wicket, but I think it's going to be very sticky. The position is, the chaps have got along alright so far without much Movement Control and aren't keen to start. I was too tired to do more than call on the Brigadier and walk round a little, and I'm very much alone in the big city. Hotel food excellent, caviar, filet a la creme, cherries and coffee plus Persian beer for dinner, but water-supply and sanitation pretty frightful.

18/6/42
It'll take a little time to get going, but then it will be a really fascinating job. I shall be the main intermediary with Bill's friends *(the Russians)*, all of which will be most instructive. I believe they're absolute bastards to deal with. But it's going to be fun.

June 21, 1942 the Allies surrender Tobruk. We were always told that if Jack had not had Jaundice he would have been in Tobruk and killed alongside most of his regiment.

22/6/42
I've got a Captain Robbins attached to me, who speaks Russian and Polish and knows Russia well, having been there before and during the last war, and most years since in business. He's quite nice and well informed, but 48 or so, and I'd much sooner have someone younger and more elastic who knew less. But I think he'll be alright.

2/7/42
The most interesting thing here is that Bill's friends are, so to speak, the chief customers. They seem to be very sticky and narrow-minded, but I feel confident, probably wrongly, that by a

little bullying I can make them less so. I haven't met them yet, so I don't know. But it's nice to see an occasional red star in the streets. They seem a tough and simple lot.

12/7/42

I've also made good contact with the UKCC. They've got a new transport man called Hayward. Oddly enough I met him in a bar in Baghdad and we both criticized the way the Russians had been handled and both said how much better we would do it ourselves. Now here we are trying to do it, which is amusing.

17/7/42

I am going south again to-morrow for two days, so I will write you a long one in the train again. I've suddenly run into being intensely busy and quite unable to get thro' the day's work, which is a very good thing. Reggie paid a lightning and very exhausting visit, seemed quite pleased with the start we're making, confirmed that there will be an extra pip in it (when, I don't know) and was altogether fun. I've had two or three talks with Bill's friends and think I'm going to like them. They are exacting but I think they have a right to be.

In the train again. Second stop. I spent the last period talking to one of Bill's friends, an army engineer. He has a rather charming interpreter with him who speaks well, and has never spoken to an Englishman before. They're rather sweet, quite excited about the journey and a bit nervous about "all these tunnels". I'm very pleased with the way my relationship with these chaps is developing. I've had a good many meetings with them now, and they accept me as the relevant person as far as they are concerned. Between you and me I'm rather pleased with my start. Brigadier Rhodes, the Director of TN, is essentially a gentleman, and tho' he never has understood what Movement Control is and cannot understand why it is necessary, once the decision had been made to establish it on him he accepted and gave every help.

A small thing happened which pleased me very much yesterday. Robbins and I were having a meeting with Bill's friends, and they returned to the fact that they were not really satisfied with the figures of the traffic moved. I explained that I wasn't in a position to answer them yet, and that my first job was to arrange for accurate and up to date information, and that I was really hoping to get going quite soon. The Colonel (they are mostly colonels) said that the General, whom I had met with Reggie, had been favourably impressed by my business like attitude and hoped that my presence would make a real difference.

There's a boy outside singing very well. The Persians go in for a very elaborate series of falsetto trills which I like.

20/8/42

The Russians burst into song last night and sang (the last thing I should have expected) the Volga Boat Song.... The Russians are very shocked at the poverty of the Arabs down here. It is perhaps the worst poverty in the world --- no food, no water, no clothes. It's obviously worse than anything they've seen in Russia.

27/8/42

It's far from good at the moment. Bill's friends have a legitimate grievance, as they are not getting enough. The whole issue is complex with many really sticky problems. But you can guess, I have only one object and that is Uncle Joe. Fischer's book shakes one a bit about him, but the perfectly normal and straightforward attitude of those chaps restores my confidence to some extent. It's all fascinating, and fully occupies every ounce I have to give, but I am far from satisfied. And so are they, and I think they are right. But don't read this as an attack on our people for not doing enough. It's more complicated than that

HQ Movement Control, Persian L of C.   19/9/42

We've now been detached from Middle East Command, which was too far away. Brigadier Rhodes is going down to HQ to be in charge of Movements and Transportation in Iran and Iraq. Reggie will be D. Movements. I'm sorry he didn't get the top job, as he's the best man there, but I've a great admiration for old man Rhodes.

I had a good trip south, and shot over to Basra with McCrudden, and spend the night with Reggie. Krasnov and I shared a carriage back in the train. His chief is Mikoyan, who is, he says, Joe's right hand man. He was a political commissar in the Finnish war. The PC *(Political Commissar)* explains everything to the troops as they go, lives with them and looks after them, and is generally father. He always has to be in the worst part of the line when they're forward. He said one man refused to have an anaesthetic unless he held his hand during the operation. We discussed discipline. He said they sent anyone who gave trouble straight to the front. But very few did as everything had been explained to them, so that they understood the difficulties and hardships.

3/10/42

I've just come thro' a very bad period. I had to prepare a plan for the Russians, and we always have a dreadful worry over that, as you must give them as much as humanly possible, but it's no good offering far more than you can ever do. Then the railway is not working as it should, so they won't even get what they ought to. And they argue like hell, and I'm inclined to think they're right, and yet I can't do any more, and so I get depressed and miserable. You see, I have to account to the Russians for all our shortcomings everywhere, and attack them for theirs, which are not negligible, and it's very wearing. The whole planning has been half-baked, really, and it's our fault we're not doing better. But in about two months we shall be doing well, and I doubt very much if their end will stand up to it.

7/10/42

Reggie is coming up with us on Saturday and we're going to give a party for our Transport Russians. Bos *(Monck)* is bringing the Minister and we shall get all the grands we can, and then get tight first and make it a party. We shall have lashings of caviar and vodka and a violin and accordion in the gallery. R & B and I will put up £10 each, and Gifford will give us £20 from his entertainment allowance at Kuibishev which he never spends. I hope it will be fun. Meanwhile Stalingrad stands, and I think it is now obvious that it will stand.

13/10/42

The party was very much OK. We got two bands in the end and a real lot of caviar and loads of drink and it swung very well. We had about 20 Russians, and every single one was blind. Some 70 to 80 people in all. One very satisfactory episode. Bos went to the Public Relations bureau and asked for pictures of Joe, Winnie and FDR as decoration. The head man refused, and told his subordinate (who passed it on) that he didn't see why he should as he hadn't been asked. Bos, white with rage, went to Reggie, who was going to see the Minister, who at once rang up the PR chap and told him to supply. He argued, and the Minister replied "Look here, I'm going to this party and I want the pictures to be there."

It started at 7 pm, and soon warmed up and by 9 o'clock we were having Russian songs and solo dances. The M. was there and saw, probably for the first time, how to throw a party for the Russians.

15/10/42

On the whole, a successful week with Reggie. We went to see the Russian general at 10 o'clock this morning. These meetings are always much the same lay-out, with Doronin (no.2) and Parankonski the interpreter, and Robbins, our interpreter, myself, our guest, whoever he may be and the General. I was thrilled, because neither Parankonski nor Doronin made it. I heard the General send for them both.

So much for our party, which we thought effective. Quite a good meeting, and at the end the general made a little speech to Reggie. Krasnov said "Let me interpret this" and said the general had said that, since I had been there they felt proper attention was being paid to their office and they found any requests or suggestions quickly met, and in fact were pleased. I said "thanks, we think our side very far from satisfactory, but with the help of my brigadier, who will always back me from Baghdad, we are trying to make a really effective show of it."

20/10/42

I was thinking, how completely one has changed, from an ordinary Movements officer to a stores for Russia maniac. What I like about it is that I am fully extended and know I'm wasting nothing of energy or brain, in fact haven't enough of either, to do the best possible.

2/11/42

We're beginning to feel the pinch of war sharply here now. It's practically impossible to get caviar, and even beer is getting scarce. Luckily there's plenty of wine, so we manage.

October/November, 1942, Allies fight and take El Alamein

2/11/42
Lt.Colonel JGS Donaldson RE

Note from the above: it's through at last. Dated with effect from 24th August.

Davidson, also Lt.Col., brought it yesterday. He is going to be in charge of Ahwaz and the ports and he and I will run the show together.

Operation Torch, the US invasion of North Africa, began on November 8, 1942.

9/11/42

Hooray, the Yanks have invaded Africa. Isn't it splendid --- action all along the line and the initiative with us at last. It's marvellous to feel things are happening at last. I asked Doronin, our no 2 Russian after the General, to come and see the Great Dictator. He and Vorobei and Parachonski the interpreter came. We got a kilo of caviare for a pound (it's obtainable again now) and two bottles of whisky, which we gave them before the film.

Afterwards Doronin insisted on a restaurant. As we'd eaten basically nothing but caviar this seemed a good idea. A lot more vodka, beer, food as required --- I must say they have great presence with the lower orders --- the old regime must have been superb if the new one is as good as this. He paid the bill without looking at it, with a thousand Real note, all splendidly in the old manner. Then the band stopped by about 11, as there's a curfew at midnight. Doronin called them all back and made them play Russian songs for ½ an hour, and then never tipped them. An amusing evening, but what impressed me was the way everyone treated them like old Russian princes.

22/11/42

Reggie has gone bear-shooting with the Russians. He's off somewhere in the mountains. He'll love it and it'll do him good. I'm also very pleased for the glory of it, as there's no other British officer in any walk of life on that sort of terms.

24/11/42

Since writing yesterday the face of the world has changed again in our favour. Krasnov rang me up at 9 o'clock and told me of the Russian breakthrough at Stalingrad, 30 miles wide and 70 deep, 13,000 prisoners and 14,000 dead.

Reggie had a most amusing, strenuous and exciting time shooting with the Russians. They started at 7 pm, drove till about 11 pm, then chased anything that showed in the headlights. If a fox or a jackal you chased it in a jeep, bending and twisting with it at 40 mph over pot-holes and water-courses. If a boar, you saw its eyes, immediately switched the car to put it in the headlights, jumped out and aimed at it with a rifle. By this time it would be going like hell, so the car would dash after it to keep it in the headlights, jinking with it and you firing from where you got out, more likely to hit the car than the boar. The final walk-up was conducted with 3 Russian rifles, 1 tommy-gun, 1 automatic pistol and 1 British rifle (Reggie's).

21/12/42

I'm immensely busy now, with four away ill. News still good. Krasnov rang me at 8.10 yesterday morning with news of the latest advance on the left bank of the Don.

20/1/43

I had a busy day yesterday, starting off by arranging a sitting with the Russian General for Parade (a Middle East weekly), and possbily Picture Post to photograph us all sitting round planning aid to Russia! I got a couple of Americans and Sinclair (UKCC) and the Russian General and Doronin. Unfortunately Krasnov was away. The chap took 60 photographs of a genuine discussion and was highly delighted. So even if they don't publish we shall probably get some prints for our own amusement, and I'll send them on.

He labelled a copy of this photograph as follows: Head of the table, facing the photographer: General Korolev; with their backs to us: Colonel Doronin and interpreter Robbins; the 3 at the left end of table: Sinclair(UKCC), Jack, Maston (USPGSC); at right hand end of table: Hart(TN); with pipe Clotz(US). Portraits of Lenin & Stalin on the wall.

24/1/43

The day before yesterday the Russians insisted on seeing General Selby, who was up, and General Connolly, from J's side. So we all troop off a 10 o'clock, and they got two hours of what we get twice a week, which I thought only fair and a good thing. Then the Russians, having had their fun, said, "And now we will have a Russian lunch". So at 11.45, much to everyone's surprise, we went to the next room, where we found a table laden with every sort of luxury. They entirely cover the table as they keep handing round other things. Vodka was pushed round, pretty fast. Klientsov, who is Krasnov's boss from Moscow, has taken rather a fancy to me, because I succeeded in getting them some tyres, so I sat next to him, and opposite both generals, next to one another. Selby obviously meant to begin by not drinking much, but, as is always the way with the Russians, he just had to.

They always get you, because, just when you've given way for the last time on the vodka and think you've just made it, they bring out Russian champagne, and give a toast and tumblerful all round and then say "Bottoms up". It's fun with us, particularly after the day's work, but a new and somewhat unexpected experience for two generals in the middle of the day.

25/1/43
Going on with the story, it was impossible not to drink a good deal, and everyone started making speeches which, owing to the boredom of having them translated, no-one was ever allowed to finish. Klientsov, who I was sitting next to, kept saying in a loud voice, "I want to see you a general" and roaring with laughter. Then, as I'd of course roped the Russians into my campaign for going home, at the end of a long and passionate peroration by Zorin, who got more boring and repetitive as the party wore on, which finished with "and help the Red Army to bring about the humiliating defeat of Hitler and bring this war to an end", Klientsov's piping voice added "so that Colonel Donaldson can go home to his family".

The Minister is mentioned several times, but I have no idea who he was and Google doesn't help.

5/2/43

I dined with the Minister last night. Whenever I go there talk always drifts to Bill's friends. Fundamentally I love them and he (the Minister) hates and despises them.

I expect you'll have got my letter by now telling you of General Selby's attempt to sack me. I've thought a good deal about it and reckon it out as follows:

1. I am an avowed socialist, and am known to be very close with the Russians. Tho' this is alright, it is perhaps a little unwise as a set-up from his point of view, as I might cheat.

2. I've too much influence here to be safe, unless his own hand-picked man. In other words, I'm just right for Reggie, as I know his mind and know just how far to go. But I'm not one of Selby's hand-picked, and I think it's quite fair that he should ge a little uneasy about me.

3. If you are energetic and generally helpful, you get people coming to you and your nose into things in just such way as you do if you are a busybody trying to build up a position for yourself. I think he thinks I'm the latter. And that is the only possible explanation of flying into a rage and taking very drastic action over what is quite obviously ridiculous triviality. I'm beginning to feel quite final about leaving this place fairly soon anyway, and can even imagine coming home.

8/2/43

Geoffrey *(? Poole, his brother-in-law)* turned up and we lunched and I told him the whole saga about Selby. He saw my letter which was perhaps rather strong and amounted to a mild indiscretion. He thinks I've had too many people giving me a crack-up, which annoys and finally produces a sort of jealousy. Soldiers are very jealous of power and position. It may be right.

I still don't know what's happened about it. I suppose I shall get a note from Reggie in the next air-mail. Selby's not a man who finds it easy to retract, so it may still be on.

The news is unbelievable. Krasnov rang up yesterday to say they were fighting in the streets of Rostov. The Boches will never recover from this. I do wish we would strike before the Russians have done all the work. Don't worry in any way about my contretemps. Reggie is such a tiger he will put it alright for me and probably make it better than if it hadn't happened.

10/2/43

There have been some developments in my saga. Robin Hankey First Secretary here, rang me up, and asked if I could see him specially. He said "We've made a blob". I said "You mean I've made a blob". He said "No, we've made a blob". He then showed me a letter from the head man to his boss, saying a certain letter had been most unfortunately circulated, signed by one of his officers without his knowledge etc. etc.

Robin then showed me his boss's draft reply, but made me swear not to say to anyone that I'd seen it. I shan't, except to you. This said that they thought the correction of the consul's statement made by me needed to be made as his statement was improper, that my letter was direct to them and was never intended to be published as a letter from me but as a correction from them, that they thought they had made a mistake in circulating it for which they were sorry, that they hoped the incident would not rebound to my discredit as they had the highest opinion of my abilities and had found me consistently helpful in giving information etc and particularly useful in dealing with the Russians.

Anyway, this will go back to our headman from Robin's headman and I imagine will calm things down somewhat Anyway I was gratified at the way they handled it and we had a good laugh all round.

11/2/43

I must see you soon. I'm beginning to think of you only as a personality I write to, and that's not right.

19/2/43

We had a most successful improvised party for Russians, Americans and Poles two nights ago. We had the Russian General, five other officers, Klientsov and Krasnov, ten in all. Then fifteen Americans and four Poles and a lot of our colonels and brigadiers who were up here for a conference. We taught the waiters at the club how to mix a gin and orange, namely half and half, and had 40 or 50 glasses ready mixed so no-one had to wait for a drink. The Russians got the form at once and started drinking well, and the whole thing went down a swing. These mixed parties always please me as I don't think they'd happen if I hadn't been here to get the relations right.

My crisis about the letter passed without event beyond a letter of reproach which was quite justified. But it was quite good in many ways. The Minister rang me up personally and said "I'm so sorry about the mess we've got you into," which I thought was very friendly.

8/3/43

I got some letters from you yesterday, 29th January to 2nd February --- very overworked and gloomy. It's rather dreadful, isn't it, that you should be slaving your guts out in the wilderness, while I live on the fat of the land and traipse about from amusement to amusement. But one can't really do anything about it, for the first four months I was here I went out very little and made no effort whatever to do anything but my work. But you gradually make friends and the circle gradually grows till you find yourself really rather social. (For instance, I'm going to a "cocktail buffet" with the Chinese Minister this evening.) Then people come up from Baghdad a lot and one has to take them out a bit.

I shall not change my rather expensive nature, I suppose, and I shall always spend more money than I ought. But as long as I have a wife to keep me I shall be alright. You say you're nervous I shan't find you as perfect as I seem to think you are, that your real achievement may be less than I think it is and so on. No. The impressive thing is the moral achievement, quite irrespective of results. The conception of your whole life since I left you has been bold and effective, and nobody can take that away from you.

3/4/43

Bill Williams writes "You have been specially asked for, for Middle East, on a goodish job which, apart from not going home, you would have liked."

Later --- I've got it, whatever it is. It's a really active job with real soldiers and all that, and it's a colossal compliment to get it You mustn't mind it being a little more active. At my rank things are always pretty safe, and it's much better for after the war to be a wee bit more in it than I have so far. It's bad, very bad, not making home, but honestly I'm so pleased about being picked out of the whole Middle East and Paiforce for a job of this kind that I can forgive them a lot. I don't know any more to tell you, but the lay-out is fairly obvious. Things are going to happen, and I'm going to be in them.

7/4/43

On Monday the new C in C was visiting, and I had to lunch at the Legation and take him to see the Russian General afterwards. It was a deeply embarrassing meeting, as they had just heard I was being whisked off, and the General and Krasnov and Klientsov talked to him about me for ½ an hour, asking that I should be left. Old Selby was there too, and it must have given him some idea of the row there would have been if he <u>had</u> sacked me. I was much embarrassed and somewhat moved. Sheridan gave a farewell party for me and the General, Klientsov and Krasnov and three more Russians came. The General made a really sweet speech about me, to which I replied saying that Churchill, Stalin and Roosevelt seemed to be able to work together alright, and we had proved <u>we</u> could work together, and as the whole future of the world depended on it it was up to us to see that American, Russian and British relations were always as cordial as they were in this room to-night. It went down very well.

12/4/43

I'm kicking my heels in Baghdad waiting for a plane to Cairo. I was very sad leaving the Russians. I went to say goodbye to Krasnov and Klientsov the night before I left. I went at 8, and they kept me till 9.30 when a terrific champagne supper was revealed next door. During this long talk a lot of interesting things were said. Krasnov talked about his boss, Mikoyan, and said "Of course he knows all about you. We used to wire 'Colonel Donaldson' but now we just wire 'Donaldson'. We shan't forget all this. It is the only important place where British and Russians meet, and it has been an experience for us". They felt very bitterly, before I got there, that they were dealing with second-raters, and it did real harm. Reggie, by putting McCrudden at Ahwaz and me at Tehran, put that right. I had a wonderful time at Tehran, and I'm damn glad to go.

5: Cairo, planning for Italy

15/4/43

Back again at Shepheard's for a couple of days. David McKenna travelled with me. Here I find Bos, on a short job before going home. My own timing is very good. I'm one of two, of which George Luck is the other, and it's quite first-class. I like being picked out like that. John Lee, who was with me at Abancourt, is on the same thing, and various others. I go on a course for four days, then back here. Going into GHQ to report, I saw on a door "Capt.Lady Sidney Farrer". My first cousin, Sidney Hobart-Hampden as was. Tell Aunt Isy. I've asked her to lunch to-morrow. Last night Bos and I dined with Patricia Kinross, Christopher Sykes and Eddie Gathorne-Hardy (do you remember him? a cousin of Ralph's, and the origin of "Lady Gertrude to you".) To-night we dine with David McKenna, who's staying with his aunt who's married to General Freyburg.

21/4/43

Nothing has happened since I wrote to you yesterday. I sat next to a Major General and an Admiral at lunch (quite by mistake, I may say) and shocked them rather by cracking up the Russians. Both these chaps were genuinely surprised, and not displeased. When chaps like that hear from people like me adequately disguised as Lt. Colonels that the Russians are bloody good and altogether charming to deal with, and that I've doing it for a year so they can't say I don't know what I'm talking about, --- well, I think it does them good and may even sink in a bit. So much for my peace effort. The Russians, I am absolutely convinced, long for peace, to get on with their own job. But they're not prepared to be pushed around or slighted and those seem to me the two things we are determined to do, and inevitably will do, unless we choose chaps like us to do it.

24/4/43

My job has changed from a more to a less active one, not less responsible but far safer. So you'll like that, tho' I'm disappointed. Reggie has been summoned for the same job, which is great fun, as I shall be under him again.

10/6/43

Note that in future my address will be Mov & Tn Twelfth Army.

This was actually meant as code for the 8th Army, but Frankie didn't understand. So she wrote to him c/o Twelfth Army (which was a German army) and not surprisingly he did not get the letters.

23/6/43

The work has been really fierce and I feel washed out and physically exhausted. I feel I'm in need of some of those Iron Jelloids which used to be advertised on the stairs of the tube at Kensington High Street, where I used to go to visit my father's Aunt Augusta. I've always had an idea of what it must feel like to be in need of Iron Jelloids, and now I've got it and I was quite right, that is just what it does feel like.

This was planning the Sicily invasion, which, probably thanks to Operation Mincemeat (The man who never was etc) came off almost without opposition.

29/6/43

Instead of easing off work has been worse and worse and has been at its climax to-day.

6: Italy and up through Europe

2/7/43
The Allies land in Sicily

We're on the move, so I've a bit of time to write. This letter will probably be held up till events have broken, when you'll know as much as I do. I've left £10 with Bill Williams to send you stockings and sweets. I've also explained to him his duties in relation to you that you are quite happy getting no news so long as you know you'll get bad news promptly.

It seems clear from the following paragraphs that Jack fully expected to be killed in the Sicily/Italian invasion. This was the last letter Frankie would have received in that event – reminding her of all the good times in their 4 years together before the 4 years of war. It is hard to read as full of undecipherable references, but I have included it as it illustrates not merely his fear about the coming action, but his concern for her, and desire to leave her with good memories and feelings in the event of his death (which he doesn't actually mention but I am certain of his state of mind at that moment). Fortunately it all went without a hitch.

Think what we've got behind us. Remember the dogs and the cottage, early Peckham, Trepp or whatever her name was and how she dropped Thomas, that ghastly time over his heart, all the fun and fight over the Wood House, Gropius, Proskauer, the Millers, Walter Goetz, Night & Day and the gramophone records, our intense political activity (!), the Sevenoaks Labour Party (no, the Ightham, wasn't it?), old Fever as the most prominent member --- your candidature as Labour member of East Malling, and that absurd and surprised clergyman --- the Left Book Club and that awful Munich morning when we sent the children away --- Higgins going to America ---- anti-Chamberlain meeting at the

Bat & Ball --- parties with the Cazalets --- drunken ham and eggs at the Wood House --- our brief career as successful golfers --- gardening and gardening again, --- Pegy's --- Witherslack --- Freddie buying all the champagne in Cromer and saying "It's your own fucking father-in-law "--- films together, plays together, music together --- Traviata, which brings me nearer to you than any other music --- jazz --- JackTeagarden --- he's the only music which can rival Traviata for producing you for me --- the Abdication and arguments with Thelma, Victor and Gladwyn Jebb --- politics, saying to Colin Coote "I'm afraid I was rude last night" and his replying "not rude, assertive and wrong" --- that marvellous golf match where we beat up him and Thelma --- Michael Bingham and sandwiches in the car in the wood near the golf course --- I can taste them now,--- and above all and everything, having you to talk to, to sulk with, to laugh with, to sit and read a book with, to sleep with, to love and to live and behalf of --- that was our life and I only live for it again. Do you remember Thomas putting his head round the door and saying "Abercrombie?" and our dreadful married couples, and going into the Wood House before it was finished, and my liverish rage when the coffee was cold? Do you remember your stamping along in the rain by the side of the car and my handing you an umbrella and its getting broken? And long long evenings with the doctors? and Geoffrey and Barbara being cross because were late for our own Xmas dinner? And then my driving off to the war with Gibby, and that last night on the sleeping porch, and you crying by the door --- and those bad days at that frightful camp, perhaps the worst of the lot for you --- and that first terrific meeting in the Minx at Dover on my first leave --- and its going slightly wrong the second time --- and our farewell party with the Cazalets and Aidan and that absurd comedian with a straw hat --- and then that frightful parting in the snow on the way to the Darlington period, and the partings in the train at Derby and then again in the cinema --- and I remember so well seeing Thomas stumping off to school with his gas mask, the last sight I had of him ---.

HQ *Movement Control 7N* Eighth Army   10/7/43

The news is out on the wireless this morning, so you now know as much as I do. I'm sitting in Frank's tent, setting off for the party in about ½ hour. Nice to be seen off by Frank *(Margesson, his cousin)*.

17/7/43

This is the first letter from Europe --- quite an occasion. I won't say where I am but if you don't know you must be stupider even than the censors.

I got into a ship the night before the assault, got out to hear the news of the assault the first day, left that night, arrived the following day, stayed on board 24 hours and finally disembarked over a beach on the third day. It was wonderful steaming into sight of land on the morning of the second day, and seeing ships and crates and everyone unloading like mad, pouring an army into Europe. And all as quiet and peaceful as a Sunday morning at Runton.

There were interruptions later on, of course, and before, but not at that particular moment, and it was quite an emotional experience. The first two days after landing were very exciting, rushing round trying to get railways and things going. Now it's less fun as everyone else has arrived, but it's still going to be fun alright, I think. There's every reason to be extremely optimistic. I shan't write a lot for the moment. We've no lights or facilities and it makes it a little difficult. It's nice to be in Europe.

18/7/43

All very well --- pretty busy. The party is quite exciting. I had a lovely Mediterranean bathe at lunch-time. Nothing to say --- my mind is full of work. I can never write well till I've settled down in my job, and I haven't altogether yet, hence a very scrappy letter.

23/7/43

It's 7 am on a lovely morning. All goes well here. I don't like being at a Head Quarters, but I'd rather be here doing this than anywhere else doing other things. The country is very fair, tho' a bit barren, the weather at this time of year sticky, the people rather charming, thoroughly co-operative and rather cowed. The whole thing is very interesting and rather fun; the war is moving quite quickly, and one does feel mildly relevant to it.

24/7/43

Feeling a little gayer to-day. Work is beginning to settle down into more normal Movement Control, which I know about and have organized before. The one tragic thing about this place is that the flies are as bad as in Egypt. How I long for the comparative immunity of England. I see the Americans have got Palermo, and I hope this stage of war will be over quite soon.

My only trouble here is that my companions are somewhat below par. The Colonel, tho' efficient, is really a pretty dreadful creature, humourless, bad-tempered and ugly. One of my contemporary Lt. Colonels is an old girl of 45, who puts his head on one side and makes frightful jokes and talks so slowly it's hard not to be out of the room before he's finished his sentence. My own particular major is better and is fun, but is a odd one, too. He's a dissipated type of ladies' man, with a drawl and all that, but has a real sense of humour, lots of guts and push, and could be a lot worse. But he's one disadvantage --- he smiles too broadly and lowers his eyelids at the same time, a dreadfully affected trick which makes me quite unable to look at him for long. I'm sure it's time I came home. I could never work with anyone but you without getting to hate the sight of them.

Same night. I'm duty officer, but there's no light so I've only got another five minutes before it's too dark. There's a sirocco on at the moment, so that, altho' it's 9 pm and the sun has been down for some time, I'm sitting drenched in sweat. Work is going better and I'm enjoying it more. I personally am full of optimism all round.

28/7/43

A chance to send this away quickly, so I take the opportunity. Things are looking up. We'll have them out very soon now. All possibilities of change, particularly rapid change are good. The thing I'm frightened of is getting settled down here. The great secret is to keep moving, I'm sure that is the best way home. Phil Dunne blew in yesterday. He's quite near here, with Bob, and I hope to get over to dinner one day. Of all people Leonard Joseph turned up as a full Lt in Movement Control. So I've roped him in to our shipping office.

30/7/43

(Heavily censored).. I've managed to acquire a jeep, which is a joy to drive, and I now bathe every morning before breakfast. Work is beginning to fall into shape.

HQ Mov & Tn Fortbase CMF   4/8/43

Note change of address. This means that we are left somewhat behind our army, but move forward with it. I can now tell you something of the past bit of history. The two months in Cairo were hell, as they were planning and planning and making preparations for the party, while conditions kept changing so that every arrangement had to be amended and amended again. The planning was done in England, N. Africa and Cairo, which made it more difficult. It was a dreadfully trying and tiring job. But great fun to see it actually happen. It was a triumphant and unqualified success, even tho' there wasn't much opposition.

5/8/43

I got in, not at the assault, but the next day, and it was all rather exciting, particularly the first sight of land at dawn. I can't describe much detail because of our delightful censors, but it was just what one would visualise, which increasingly I find life always is. With this big difference --- we had expected many difficulties, and found very few.

6/8/43

It's difficult to write as there's so little time. I'm just sneaking ten minutes before the morning bathe. It's the only thing that keeps me alive --- this place is frightfully relaxing, hot and sweaty --- I'm sure my liver is in a bad way. I had lunch with Phil two days ago. They've got a nice house and a good cook. Reggie is now installed here at 21 Army Group, which is the commanding formation of Eighth Army and US Seventh. Things are full of interest and action here, and I'm not too bored. I don't last more than about three or four weeks at a job now without going off a bit, which I suppose is what is known as war-weariness.

This letter has taken me three days and now I have missed the post. But things are moving fast.

8/8/43

Your description of Rose is great fun. They seem to be growing up pretty decent, thanks to your influence and neglect, by which I mean thank goodness you've never had time to pamper them.

I'm fantastically busy again, and happier in my work, tho' it's not really my sort of stuff, but I seem to have got stuck pretty badly in HQ now. However, this is a quick moving stage of the war, and I can accept any job for a month or two.

18/8/43

I see now from orders I'm allowed to tell you I'm in Sicily, and came here from Malta. We came over from Malta in a very fast minelayer, and we picked up the crew of a Flying Fortress on the way, and were at the same time attacked, very briefly, by a Boche plane. Quite exciting for about four minutes, then over --- no more thrills.

The concentration of the invasion fleet was one of the most extraordinary feats of naval warfare. We saw most of the ships, coming from our side, on the way out, and they met the others coming from elsewhere perfectly to time, drew up in position for assault and then assaulted all in some unbelievable way without the Boche knowing what it was all about. And the final assault achieved surprise, a thing no-one had thought possible.

I left Malta the day after the assault, but hung about here for twenty four hours before we could get off. It was all fairly exciting, and extremely successful. I feel things are on the move all the world over. I begin to visualize the three weeks leave we are entitled to after more than two years abroad.

21/8/43

We moved up the day before yesterday. Our new mess is rather a nice modern villa, with a bath and electric light, both working. This is a great joy, as usually light and water-mains have been bombed and not yet mended. We live on the outside of the town with a fine view of Etna. This morning the owners of the villa, who are frightfully pleased because we have let them stay in the bottom rooms instead of turning them out altogether, brought up a lovely plateful of bright green figs.

22/8/43

Frantically busy again, and getting rather tired of it all. The climate is very trying, hot, sticky and relaxing. My mind is working badly this morning. I've sat here for five minutes without thinking of anything to say. It's difficult --- I can't go on saying I think the war will be over soon, which I've said in every letter for the last two years. I can't tell you my particular worries here, which of course are what are in my mind at the moment. I've answered all the points from your letters. I'll finish to-night as I want my breakfast.

24/8/43

I got three letters yesterday. It's most amusing that you didn't know where I was. The only dangerous jobs are the actual landing, and less so, but still a little, recce parties which go in the first day. The second day, except for a few air-raids, was just like Hyde Park on a weekday morning. I didn't get kissed by the natives, but they're obsequious and enthusiastic to get a job with the British. My feeling was that they were jolly glad to get on with the peace. I agree with you about Mussolini. The complete fading out is absolute humiliation, and couldn't be better. I think it is beautiful. I got three sweet letters from Thomas. I'm glad he seems happy at school, and thinks he's good at arithmetic.

4/9/43

Now that you've seen the news of our little landing in Italy, you'll see why I've been so busy lately. I think it was three weeks of the hardest work I've ever done, but it's all gone off quite well. I've enjoyed it, at least in retrospect.

Yesterday motored up to the tip of the island to see how the traffic was going. It was nice to see Italy, and to see craft running over to it without so much as a shot fired. The first prisoners to arrive this side were a charming group who rowed the 3 1/2 miles in a boat with a white flag attached, to beg us to stop the artillery barrage. They then had to be put to bed as they were quite ill with exhaustion, and had dreadful blisters on their hands. A number of us will move on quite son and I'm determined to be one of them. I don't think home arises until the whole Italian party is over, which I think will be in a couple of months at worst. I've just talked to Army, and they tell me we've so far advanced 75 miles and found only one German!

It's lovely having Tommy *(Thomson)* here. *(They worked together in Egypt and met and corresponded after the war).* He is a real friend and such a good worker. I can leave the whole of the railway side to him and concentrate on other things, of which there are plenty.

Work has gone very fairly, and it has been quite a difficult job from the movements point of view.

8/9/43

Isn't it nice about Italy packing in? Much cheering and rejoicing in the town, which is an odd way to receive news of unconditional surrender. I suppose the Boche will fight a prolonged rear-guard action all the way up, but I should think they'll be pretty uncomfortable and go a good deal faster than without the surrender.

9/9/43

This morning the great attack in the Naples area began. No news of it yet. I hope we shall go there quite soon.

13/9/43

I have been so immensely proud of what you've done, and every one I've told about it has been so full of praise and envy, and often even said they wished their own wives had the guts to do the same. So you can feel that, to the ordinary chap I meet out here, what you have done has been almost a wish-fulfilment of his own ambitions. Everyone wants a farm after the war to go back to, and we're the only ones I know who've had the courage and brains, energy and determination, not only to get one but to make a success of it ... and write a first-class book into the bargain. I suppose I've lent the book to some 50 people, and several have read it independently.

I've never had it back without the most sincere and genuine compliments, and I feel separately proud each time. When you gloom about life, because I feel the gloom so deeply myself I realize it's worse in every single aspect for you. You've done something truly remarkable and widely recognised as such, so if you <u>can</u> keep it up till I get back, it will be all the more so.

I can only give you my absolute confidence in whatever you do. I recommend more holidays and a bit of gaiety if you can find it, and some company if you can get it. People sometimes help to pull one out of introspection and depression. What you've endured is three times longer than anything you've got to endure in the future, so keep on, darling.

15/9/43
The campaign in Italy is not going as fast as I had hoped, but still it's going. I seem to be more or less stuck with this HQ, but when we move Reggie will move with us, so it won't be so bad. We've only got one problem, waiting.

20/9/43
I haven't written for about four days, which is bad. But I hit a rush and literally had no time. I went with Marcus Sieff by air 100 miles into Italy, spent the night there, came back by various places and fetched up here 3 pm the next day. I then worked till 1.30 am, all next day, and yesterday till 1 am again. Now, having cleared that particular one, there's another coming up.

26/8/43
We're just as frantically busy now as we were in Cairo. We have split off from HQ Eighth Army as a sort of base HQ, and shall stay here for some time, tho' we shall move forward as the Army does. Tommy Thomson and Freddie Linck have both arrived. Tommy is a tower of strength. Except for about a week at the beginning, when I rushed about the country, I've sat in an office 12/14 hours a day 7 days a week ever since I arrived in Cairo, in April, and it's getting me down.

26/9/43
We've already moved part of ourselves, and I hope to go in four or five days. I had a frightful rush combined with a frightful liver attack, so haven't written much. Both are over now. Yesterday Humphrey Lomer blew in, fresh from Naples, a full of beans and argument. I was dining with Gerry Wellesley, who's the chief Amgot (Civil Affairs) officer here, and I took Humphrey along.

Humphrey asked him if he's seen his nephew the duke, whom H. knows. I piped up that Phil Dunne had told me he was killed at Salerno, thinking of course that Gerry would know. His eyes opened very wide, and he said "What" very slowly three time, and I thought "Oh, God, I've dropped a frightful brick he must have worshipped him and this is the first he's heard of it". But it soon became apparent that the paralyzing effect was produced by the fact that, if true, Gerry would succeed to the title! Quite an effective little scene, and rather an unusual one.

I shall mount my jeep in a few days and drive in a leisurely way, probably with Denis Stenhouse whom I like, over the ferry and all the way by road. I'm told that Bomber Harris beat the table with his fist and said "I'll beat the buggers by Xmas". The fall of Smolensk is a terrific blow, we're doing well in Italy, the French (the <u>French</u> mind you) have attacked the Hun in Corsica and they're being harried in Jugoslavia and must be fairly uncomfortable in Greece.

30/9/43
Just setting off for the long drive to the heel, which should be a very pleasant holiday. I took a lovely day off yesterday and went up Etna with Humphrey. The Crater was smoking in places, but otherwise quiet. We motored to within 4000 feet of the top, and then climbed for 3/3 ½ hours.

There's a lieutenant here called Stewart, who was just a name to me, and I allowed him to be one of the ones left behind. Then Leonard Joseph told me at supper he was first violin for Jack Hylton. I made him get out his fiddle (he bought one at Syracuse) and he played hot numbers with Leonard till late into the night. The annoying thing is, he's really good, and no-one knew it or anything about him. I'm mad with rage that I've let him go.

Jack's passion had always been music and he managed to set up a Quartet Society in Italy.

23/1/44

The first consignment of violin strings etc were sent off on January 6th and arrived on January 15th. I hope to start the quartet again when I get back. Unfortunately they wouldn't let poor old Baroni conduct the opera, as a tenor (a very moderate one) whom he had insulted as an artist on some occasion, denounced him as a fascist. Of course he was a fascist, poor old boy, he had to be to keep his job, and before that a Mason, and anything which got him work. It's very difficult to interfere in a case like this, even tho' I'm sure it's a nonsense.

18/2/44

We had a very good Debussy last night, but it's just as well it was the last of the first series of concerts as the audience is getting a bit thin. However, it's been great fun. We've had six concerts, and they've always been attended by about 20 Other Ranks (free) and 10 to 20 officers. The whole thing will cost me about a fiver to make up deficits. I think it's cheap at the price.

21/2/44

I went to Tosca last night --- a very decent performance.

1/3/44

The second instalment of violin strings has just arrived. I wrote to Garrett after the first. Will you thank him again? I had a sad interview with poor old Baroni yesterday. I told you he had been denounced as a fascist by a jealous tenor, and is now not allowed to conduct. He was hoping I could help him but I can't.

The first Eton Jazzband, founded by Jack as a schoolboy.

2/3/44

I went to Madame Butterfly this afternoon --- a very decent performance. I saw Angus Menzies there, of all people. He's been out a year or two, but is just moving away.

7/3/44

One good story I forgot to tell you. We went to the Royal box at the opera for Butterfly. Tommy's girlfriend Etta was the only woman, so she and Tommy sat in the central royal chairs. She said she hadn't been to the opera for five years, and when she last did go Hitler was sitting in the very same chair.

10/3/44

I've been pretty busy. Yesterday I went a tour forward to look at the battle from a safe distance with Basil Rogers. To-morrow I'm flying to Sicily for a couple of days to see how they're getting on, as they've recently come under our jurisdiction. I hope it's a bit warmer down there.

Since I've been back I've become very fond indeed of Denis Healey, who will certainly come into our lives later on. I sat up late last night discussing dialectical materialism, which he understands and I don't properly, and thence philosophy, ethics and life in general. I find his outlook and his very acute brain most congenial and am enjoying talking to him very much.

I'm going to Forza del Destino to-night. It's not often done in England. I saw it once. It's great fun hearing less well-known operas here, in fact the only worthwhile thing I can think of that ever does happen.

Back in England for a short spell, working at the War Office.

QM Main HQ 21 Army Gp 1 APDC London W1   26/4/44
It seems pretty absurd being here. We shan't be too uncomfortable in a day or two. It's a lovely park, but will get bogged down if it rains. I foresee no work to do at all, and am a little cross about it.

7: In France: D Day and after

12/6/44
So far all very well. I'm sitting in the sun on deck off the invasion coast, very peaceful and happy. More shipping around us than I've ever seen in one place in my life, and than anyone else has, I expect. We spent two days in a marshalling camp and finally got on board Sunday morning. It's unbelievable to sit here all day in this mass of shipping and never hear a gun fired. I think Monty has got his "firm base" alright. Our last two months have been a very wonderful foretaste of what is to come.

c/o Q(M) 11 L of C APO England   14/6/44
I'm having fun so far. We finally got off the boat Monday evening and slept on the ground just clear of the beaches. Off at 6 next morning and dumped Butler *(his batman)* and kit here and on to meet McKillop at another beach as arranged. Drove him round all day, and met up with my US opposite number, Bob Kyser, who came back for the night. I went round with him all day to-day, and saw quite a lot, and also bought 2 kilos of excellent Normandy butter, and discovered a Camembert cheese factory, where I ordered 20 cheeses for the mess at 8 francs each (10 francs to a shilling). Everyone seems quite happy about the battle, so who are we to worry if it seems a bit slow! Butler is turning out really good and the jeep is a dream.

28/6/44
You ask about the French. I think the locals round here have never wanted for anything, it being a rich farming country, and were physically contented under the Boche. They can hardly be that under us as we're inevitably doing great damage to the fields and have involved them in a lot of bombing. But I think they are pretty solid in being pleased, in a rather nervous sort of way, that

the German domination is over. I think they quite liked the Boche soldiers but found the head men very harsh indeed.

8/7/44

The 450 bomber raid announced this morning was the most terrific sight I've ever seen. They swarmed over, it seemed very slowly and inevitably, dropped their bombs in intense flack, turned and flew leisurely back.

23/7/44

A quick line by hand of Gerry. I did get the Order of the Patriotic War, first class. I don't know what other people got, so I don't know if it's jolly good or just quite nice. But I'm jolly pleased.

Order of the Patriotic War, First Class.
Дж. Г. С. Дональдсон

24/8/44

I saw Peter *(Cazalet)* and Anthony *(Mildmay)* and they were both in fine fettle, having had a bit of fighting and come to no harm. Anthony's best one was when, for no reason, he left his seat in the tank and sat on the floor, and a shell went through the tank and out the other side, singeing his hair only, which would have killed him if he hadn't moved.

3/9/44

Things are going so fast you won't hear from me for a bit.

7/9/44

We had a hectic and most amusing rush forward. I wrote to you last from the place where I bought the bicycle, call it A, having lunched with my old station-master at B, and having visited my old HQ town C. The next day we came up to C again, dashing out to various places north of it, and the next day to where I told Peter I would be, D. Oddly enough, he was there too, but I missed him. I go back there to-morrow to stay probably a week or two.

These notes don't quite make sense. I think he had forgotten the order in which he mentioned them by the time he wrote the decode letter, but it seems to have been Rouen, Abancourt, Amiens and Brussels.

Coming into fairly major liberated towns is most exciting. They demonstrate a lot and very nicely, all the children shouting and so on. It's even more so in Belgium, and in D the whole place was en fete. We've been from one to two days behind the Boche all the way along, and go always straight to the railways and tell them what to do. So far we have had a marvellous reception, and have got things cracking far earlier than had been expected, so much so that we're ready before our customers, which is exciting.

I've been working very intensively for the last week, and if I may say so, in my opinion John Lee and I have done jolly well, better than anyone else would have done. To-morrow we hope to see the results of our labour, in the form of trains puffing about the place. We've fairly galvanized the French and Belgians and it's been great fun.

12/9/44

I wrote to you last from Amiens, which I called B, and haven't written for some time. Since then I've been up here and down there and up here again. We got our first grain in the day before yesterday, which was quite good. I'm up here as a sort of advance section, with John Lee, Butler and Bill Hart, who was railway operating in Persia, and we're just beginning to relax after the first burst of energy in getting things going. This place, which I called C, and where I just missed Peter, is very good --- quite normal peace-time and most agreeable.

We were in Rouen twenty-four hours after capture, Amiens and here forty-eight. The day after we arrived at Rouen we went on to Abancourt. It was most dramatic. I was the last to leave the station with old Racine (the *station master at Abancourt in 1940*) four years ago, a few hours before the Boche got there, and twenty four hours after the British passed through I was the first to go into the station, four years later.

We drew up and saw one of the shunters going off on his bicycle. We yelled "Dupont, Dupont" at him, and he threw away his bicycle and rushed over and embraced us both. Then he took us round and we found Racine, just the same, very moved and a little older. He took us to lunch with his wife, who cried on my shoulder, and then gave us a whacking great lunch. We had to go on to Amiens but came back to Abancourt for tea, and I was really happy to be with them again.

The next day we moved up to Amiens to stay, and met Ian Cameron. He and John and I had all been at Abancourt together. Soon after I arrived I heard that Racine had been arrested as a collaborator --- it was then 10pm. You can imagine I felt pretty bad, but all I could do was to send John down early next morning to see what it was all about. The next day I had to go to Arras and didn't get back till after lunch when one of the railway officials told me Racine was in prison in Amiens. So Ian Cameron and I went and saw the Field Security Police and the Sureté Generale and finally the Prefet, and got his release. Ian then went to the prison to get him out, only to find that he had been released that afternoon and had caught the 6.45 to Abancourt! Ian went to see him the next day and we got the whole story, which we were able to prove with the help of the French railway filing system, and he is now I think finally exonerated.

The story was that a certain shunter was a communist, which is a slightly more questionable thing to be in France than it is in England, and had chalked up a hammer and sickle on a signal box. Racine had him up and warned him that he would get them all in trouble with the Boche if he did that sort of thing, but he did it again. This time two of his colleagues (French) complained to Racine that they were frightened to work with him. Racine then reported the matter to the French railway authorities at Amiens, who passed it to the Prefet, who passed it to the Boche, and the man was taken away to Germany, leaving a wife and three children.

Some of the station staff thought that Racine had given it straight to the Boche, hence his denunciation and arrest, but the letters we found proved he didn't, so he should be alright. However, it was rather a nasty taste all round, and brought one up short after the very moving re-union we'd had the day before. At lunch at the Racines the baker's wife came in. Her son had been a prisoner and escaped and she was pleasantly anti-German.

At Arras I met another old friend, de Villele, who was building marshalling yards for us near Abancourt in '40. He too embraced me, and I went and had an egg for my tea with him and his wife on one of my passings through. All very nice. But the further north you go, the warmer the reception, till you reach Belgium, where it is red hot.

Yehudi Menuhin is giving a recital on the 14th, which I shall try to get to. Meanwhile, I've rather changed my view about the war. I believe the buggers are going to go on fighting after we get into Germany. We've won the battle of France, and of the Netherlands (or will have soon). But the reduction of Germany, if they go on fighting, can take a long time. My hunch is now that they will.

This is very depressing. It's all worked out exactly as I'd hoped up to now, and I've had great fun and become active and energetic again. But now, according to my plan, they should stop and pack in. And I'm not at all sure they're going to. And I don't much fancy a winter in a hostile Germany, with no houses standing and an embittered people all round us. That's all my news. I wish I could have some of yours. I'm anxiously waiting to hear what has happened about the farm. I think communications should get right in about a week.

As usual he was over-optimistic about the ending of the war. On September 17 Operation Market Garden began and ended in disaster, delaying the end of the war considerably.

15/9/44

We're settling in nicely, and not working quite so hard. We've got a radio gramophone in the flat, and by paying £2.10/ for a valve have got it working. Now we've spent £5 on records, so we're quite civilized. I bought the Petite Suite by Debussy and Carnival Romain by Berlioz, and half a dozen good jazz records. The Dutch and Belgian bands are quite good. Of course Coleman Hawkins and Benny Carter played in Holland for some time before the war. We asked where to go to hear a good band, and they told us Le Boeuf sur le Toit. So John and I took Eric Sandars there last night, and it was really a very fair band.

The place was crowded out and very hot, and nine drinks cost nearly £4. We asked a couple of Belgians next to us if it was always like this, and they said under the Boche there were never more than ten or twenty people, and that <u>no-one</u> went out. They also said that they had been pretty continuously drunk since the liberation and so had everyone else, and we could never know what it meant.

18/2/45

We had a very good trip to Abancourt. We stopped for lunch at Arras at a French Officers' mess, which was quite fun, and then on to Abancourt. We went all round the yard with Racine, and then sat down to a really Gargantuan feast. We started with small glasses of Calvados as aperitif, then soup of onions and potatoes and a good pint of cream, with some light port to drink. Then some very strong but excellent pate maison with guerkins, and a very good Bordeaux. Then rabbit cooked with mushrooms in brandy and some delicious sweet cyder. Then a pause and the "trou Normand", a couple of glasses of really beautiful old Calvados. Then a colossal turkey with some more Bordeaus. Then a custard tart which melted in the mouth, washed down with a beautiful but slightly sweet Sauterne. And before that some really delicious Neufchatel cheese, related to Cambembert but eaten fresh. After the tart a gateau chocolat and more Sauterne. Then nuts and champagne, then brandy and coffee, then a sweet liqueur (God knows what) then more Calvados and more champagne. We sat down at 7 and got up at 12.15 and finally left at 2 am. The Racines, the Bouchers (he was the proprietor of the cafe where we messed) and "Daisy" the waitress, and the baker's daughter and the farmer's daughter and another niece of Madame's and Grand'mere Boucher and a little sister of one of them aged 3, and our Belgian chauffeur and four of us.

Quite incredible after four years of occupation. But of course it is a rich farming country and they'd been preparing it for three or four days. But it was a very great occasion. I only wish our two French officers, Sanguy and Bonefon, had been there, but I had letters from both in my pocket and I made everyone sign on two bits of paper to send them one each. We got back safely about 6 and to-night I'm going to hear Trios by Beethoven and Schubert organized by the Naval Chaplain.

There were no more letters of interest and Jack returned home late summer 1945.